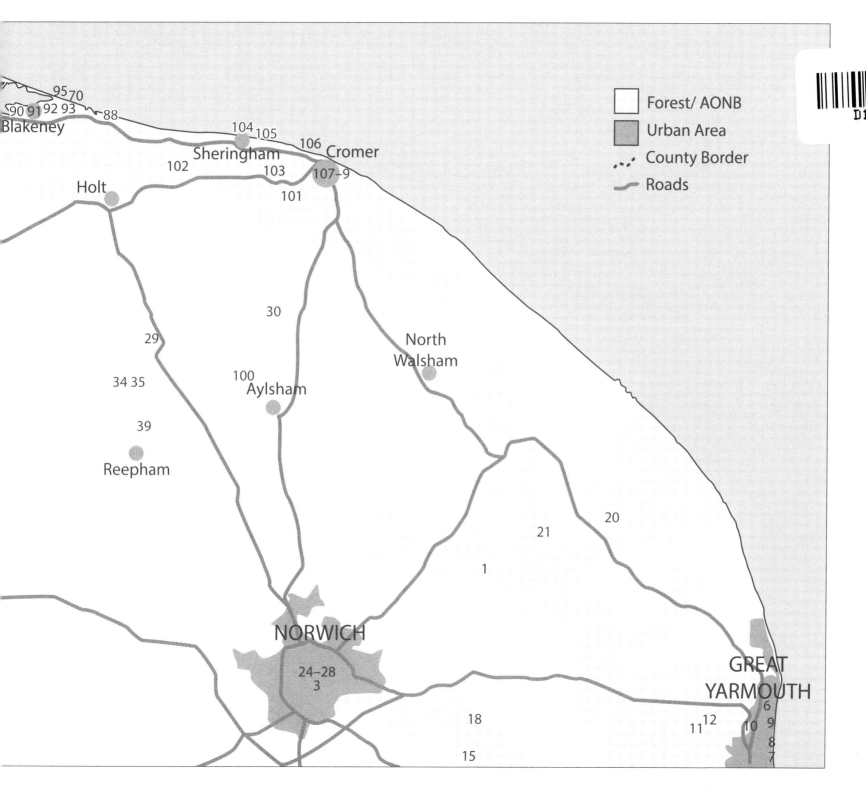

Forest/ AONB
Urban Area
County Border
Roads

Blakeney
95 70
90 91 92 93
88
104 105
Sheringham 106 Cromer
102 103 107–9
101
Holt
30
North Walsham
29
34 35
100
Aylsham
39
Reepham
21
20
1
NORWICH
24–28
3
18
GREAT YARMOUTH
6
11 12
9
10
15
8
7

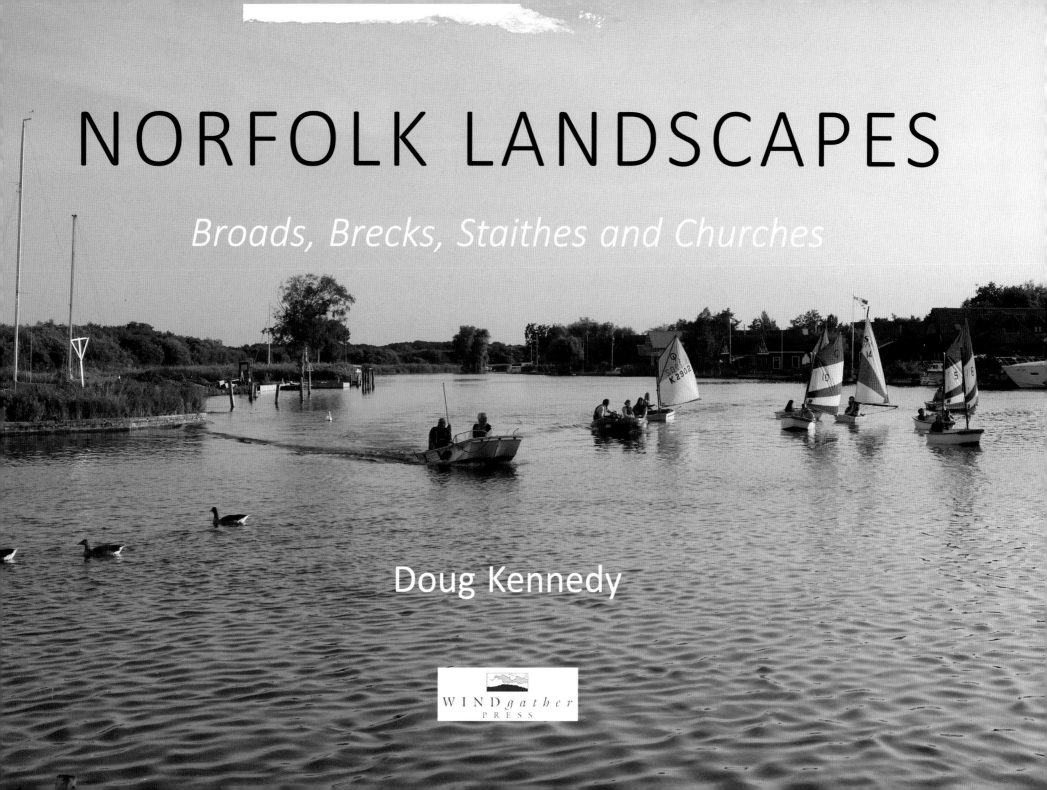

NORFOLK LANDSCAPES

Broads, Brecks, Staithes and Churches

Doug Kennedy

WINDgather PRESS

Windgather Press is an imprint of Oxbow Books

Published in the United Kingdom in 2015 by
OXBOW BOOKS
10 Hythe Bridge Street, Oxford OX1 2EW

and in the United States by
OXBOW BOOKS
1950 Lawrence Road, Havertown, PA 19083

Hardback Edition: ISBN 978-1-909686-81-6
Digital Edition: ISBN 978-1-909686-82-3

A CIP record for this book is available from the British Library

Printed in Wales by Gomer Press

For a complete list of Windgather titles, please contact:

United Kingdom
Oxbow Books
Telephone (01865) 241249
Fax (01865) 794449
Email: oxbow@oxbowbooks.com
www.oxbowbooks.com

United States of America
Oxbow Books
Telephone (800) 791-9354
Fax (610) 853-9146
Email: queries@casemateacademic.com
www.casemateacademic.com/oxbow

Oxbow Books is part of the Casemate Group

All photographs have been taken by Doug Kennedy (www.doug-kennedy.com)
apart from that of the Swallowtail butterfly on page 93, which is by Tim Melling.

Title page: An evening sailing class at Horning
Contents page: Norwich cathedral

Contents

Introduction

This book explores Norfolk in photographs and descriptive text that reveals the story behind the image. Although the County's highest point (Beacon Hill) has an altitude of only 105 metres (340 feet), Norfolk contains several distinct landscapes of great character which we visit in turn. Some of these, such as the Norfolk Broads and the North Norfolk Coast, are enormously popular as holiday destinations, whilst less well-known are the rolling sandy landscape of Breckland, the low-lying fens in the east, the gentle Waveney Valley and the agricultural centre with its great houses and pretty villages. Because the county was largely bypassed by the Industrial Revolution many towns and villages remain quite unspoilt and almost every view across the landscape contains at least one church tower.

On our journey we encounter plenty of the huge open skies that Norfolk is known for, but also pretty corners where the light somehow brightens colours and heightens the atmosphere and sense of place. We visit towns, villages, farms, waterways and the coast, seeking out scenes and features that define the location and that live in peoples' minds as icons of what Norfolk means. Wildlife thrives in the expanses of open water and countryside. Here are to be found many species of birds and dragonflies, some of which are migratory and a few that are unique to Norfolk, so several pages scattered through this book are devoted to these lovely creatures.

We start our journey at Great Yarmouth in the south-east corner of Norfolk and explore up the River Yare and the Norfolk Broads, which is a varied low-lying landscape of waterways and broads (lakes) interspersed with farms, villages and even the occasional hill. This area is a magnet for boat-lovers who can wander through the many miles of winding waterways enjoying the lovely scenery and abundant wildlife. We then go to the county town of Norwich before meandering through the central agricultural area with its huge open fields, picturesque settlements and amazing great houses whose parks, sometimes including entire villages, were often laid out by important landscape designers.

Thetford and The Brecks come next where heath, forest and twisted pines combine to make a unique landscape which is hard to farm because of the very light sandy soil. In the far south, the Waveney Valley forms the border with Suffolk and seems to take time at a slower pace than elsewhere. Then we come to the flat expanses of The Fens, which spread for huge distances to the east from Downham Market into Cambridgeshire and Huntingdonshire, cut through by the ramrod-straight rivers and drainage channels.

Finally, we visit the North Coast with its amazing coastal marshes running from Holme-next-the-Sea to Sheringham, and strung together by a series of villages, most of which were once ports but are now beloved of yachting folk, walkers and birders. Immediately behind these is a chalk ridge that includes the lofty Beacon Hill and some great panoramas northwards across the coast and also over the agricultural hinterland to the south. This elevated region is dotted with more large houses and estates with some of the loveliest parks and gardens in England.

The material for this book was collected whilst walking lengths of the Ferryman's Way, Peddar's Way, Weaver's Way, the North Norfolk Coast Path and many other footpaths and byways, seeking out scenes and panoramas that have a true sense of place. It also involved trips by car where the author was seeking out a particular feature or type of landscape, often attempting to time visits to coincide with good light. However, having the North Sea on two sides, the weather can be very unpredictable, and a fantastic light over one village may well not be replicated a few miles down the road. I once waited for hours in a freezing bird hide at Cley-next-the-Sea for the sun to appear from underneath a cloud, only to have to run for the car park through wind-blown sleet. On the other hand, the weather on the morning I took the photographs of Holkham House and Beach was dull and damp and I was about to head home when suddenly the sun burst through with spectacular results.

Of course, Norfolk has far more to offer than can be included in this book and, to a certain extent, what does appear has depended upon my happening to pass when the light was right. But the images cover the length and breadth of Norfolk at all four seasons, and have been chosen not only for their location and quality, but also for the way that they fit together visually. Hopefully this varied collection of photographs, together with the text, paints a colourful picture of Norfolk that both natives and lovers of the county will recognise and enjoy.

The Norfolk Broads and Yarmouth

We start in the south-east corner of Norfolk, on the coast at Great Yarmouth, and then wander past Breydon Water to the River Yare and into the Norfolk Broads. The Broads National Park is a mosaic of rolling landscape, lakes and rivers covering 303 square kilometres around the rivers Bure, Ant and Thurne, and extending south to the Yare, Waveney and on into Suffolk. Many of the channels and lakes result from peat digging in past centuries so are not natural landscape features; a fact that was established only in the 1960s. This national park is rich in wildlife and habitats, including 28 sites of special scientific interest (SSSI's) and a national nature reserve.

The network of waterways is a huge attraction for people who like yachting and motor cruising, as the extent of connected water is enormous and the scenery often spectacular. Many of the settlements in this area have boatyards and marinas, some of which are extensive and bring in a lot of business to this rather remote corner of England. The waterways seem crowded for only a few peak periods in the year and most of the time, you can wander in a boat or on foot for days without retracing your steps, enjoying the huge skies, stretches of water of all sizes, windmills, villages, picturesque mooring points or staithes and reed beds. It can also be worth stopping to watch a skilled yachtsman cope with the variable breezes whilst negotiating a river bend and avoiding other craft.

The waterways are only part of the story, because they are all bordered for much of their length by huge reed beds and marshes that often spread as far as the eye can see and which provide a safe habitat for many rare species of birds, fish, dragonflies and butterflies. It is well worth taking things slowly in a boat or on foot as this is the best way to absorb the atmosphere and encounter these lovely creatures.

Where the reeds and water give way to dry land, it is very fertile, so farming tends to be productive. This depends upon the management of the waterways, which has enabled the growth of a number of prosperous settlements, often with large churches, in an area that might have remained unproductive swamp.

Left: The River Chet with boats heading downstream towards the River Yare

Great Yarmouth

Great Yarmouth spreads along the North Sea coast from Gorleston-on-Sea, close to the Suffolk border, for over 4 miles, with a huge sandy beach that has long been an attraction for holiday makers. It also has a port along the mouth of the River Yare where the oldest and most interesting buildings are concentrated. It is an ancient town with a great history and in 1724, Daniel Defoe wrote that it was "..infinitely superior to Norwich..." for its wealth, trade and situation. Nowadays the once thriving herring industry is much depleted and the tourist business that fuelled the town's expansion in the twentieth century has diminished, but the town still has much to attract visitors.

There is an intriguing area around the Minster which contains a number of ancient buildings such as the medieval Fishermans' Hospital and the town wall. You will also find the indoor market (page 9) towards the middle of town. The most significant heritage area is the South Quays (page 10) which contains many historic buildings such as the Town Hall, the Old Customs House, the Nelson Museum and quays along the River Yare that are still active. Moored at the quayside you are likely to see a great variety of ships including the extraordinarily complex offshore service and supply vessels as well as cargo ships, and the last surviving herring drifter, the *Lydia Eva*.

On its east side, Great Yarmouth has an enormous beach stretching the length of the town (page 8) that is pure creamy sand without the protective groins that are so common along this coast, dividing the beaches into sections. In stark contrast to this clean simplicity, the coast is completely taken up with holiday developments that spread along both sides of the 'Golden Mile' (opposite), including two piers, amusement arcades, pubs, hotels and all the fun of the fair.

Left: A picturesque corner close to the Minster
Right: Along the Golden Mile. The beach is off to the right of this image

Overleaf Left: The beach at sunset
Overleaf Right: Inside the covered market at Great Yarmouth

Contrasting Worlds

Great Yarmouth is a busy town with quite dense housing and few green spaces, and it feels very urban. It is sandwiched between the North Sea and the River Yare which flows into the shallow lake of Breydon Water, so if you head either east or west out of the town, you abruptly find yourself in a totally different world.

To the east, the broad and open beach sands stretch from the Yare estuary for many miles northwards. Right by the town you can sit watching the North Sea waves crashing down and feel quite remote, as long as you don't turn around. A mile to the west, through the urban streets, you come to the quays ranged along the River Yare (see left), and if you follow this upstream to the train station, immediately to the west lies the wide shallow lake that is Breydon Water. This stretches into the distance, surrounded by low-lying reed beds, marshes and pasture; it is a wild place with no roads or buildings, only the huge expanse of Halvergate Marshes under an enormous sky. Following the footpath along the dyke on the north shore, all you will see on a summer's day will be birds, butterflies and the occasional cow browsing among the wildflowers. Your ears will be treated to birdsong and the wind soughing through the rushes. In fact, so few people go there that the birds seem tamer, and there can be clouds of butterflies that rise as you walk.

Whether walking or sailing out of Yarmouth up the River Yare there is no habitation for over four miles, until you reach the Berney Arms pub, which sits on a bend a little to the west of Breydon Water. As there are no roads it is effectively one of the most remote pubs in England. However, there is a railway halt a couple of hundred yards away where the train from Norwich passes once or twice a day and will stop on request. Thomas Berney insisted that the station was provided as a condition of the sale of land to the railways in 1844, a condition that remains in force to this day.

It is a lovely spot with the wide sweep of the river, the windmill (see page 13) and views towards the Burgh Castle Roman remains. The peace, only disturbed by the occasional motor launch, continues for a further 3 miles up-river to Reedham.

In the days before roads, the River Yare and other Broads rivers were the major thoroughfares, carrying goods and people mostly in wherries to and from Norwich and Yarmouth.

Left: South Quays at Great Yarmouth
Right: The fens beside Breydon Water

Overleaf Left: Looking along Breydon Water from the Peddar's Way footpath
Overleaf Right: Looking west up the River Yare from the Berney Arms

The Norfolk Broads

Continuing upstream towards Norwich along the River Yare, the land rises and marshes contract, to be replaced by fertile agricultural land and settlements. The village of Reedham sits on a little hill and marks the end of the silent expanses of marsh and the start of roads. The railway crosses the Yare here on its way to Lowestoft and the small ferry is the only vehicle and pedestrian river crossing between Yarmouth and Norwich. Without this, motor vehicles heading north or south would have a long extra journey into Norwich, 12 miles to the west.

The River Chet joins the Yare just above the ferry and there are also fingers of water which, like all the Broads lakes, were created by centuries of peat digging and subsequent inundation. Once dredged, these strips of water became navigable and now provide mooring for boats, often with a staithe at their end. The older staithes, such as that at Loddon, used to be loading points for wherries, which transported local produce and people to the towns, and without which transport would have been extremely difficult. A few wherries with their robust wooden hulls and square sails are still to be seen plying the Broads, normally as pleasure boats.

Another interesting feature of these rivers, and of the topography of the region in general, is that they often flow between dykes at a higher level than the surrounding land with the result that adjacent buildings can appear lower than passing boats (see page 16). One explanation for this phenomenon lies in the way the land has been used over the centuries. Marsh vegetation when partially decomposed creates peat. Peat is excellent for agriculture, but working the land exposes the organic material to air and the dormant process of decomposition is reawakened, resulting in a gradual drop of the land level. In low-lying areas such as the fens where the land has fallen below sea level, water has to be constantly pumped away into the rivers and drainage channels, and this in turn explains the presence on the Broads of windmills, which are in fact wind-driven water pumps. Nowadays electric pumping stations do the job and the windmills are idle.

Left: Agricultural land along the Yare at Hardley Street, with St Margaret's church tower on the left

Right: Rockland Staithe: This landing place was once used by wherries to transport locally made tiles to market. The wooden structure is the frame of a wherry that has been partially buried to recall those times

Overleaf Left: A yacht on the River Yare appears to be sailing through the dry land
Overleaf Right: A house built below the level of the river

Nature in The Broads

One of the great joys of gently cruising through The Broads is the wildlife that you encounter on the way. There are almost always birds, such as swans, ducks, herons, grebes and gulls on the water and large flocks of geese abound whilst warblers, buntings and bitterns call from the reed beds and marsh harriers glide overhead. In the summer, there are many colourful dragonflies and butterflies, including some spectacular local specialities such as the Swallowtail butterfly and the Norfolk Hawker dragonfly (see left). If you are very lucky, in some quiet places along the muddy river banks you might glimpse an otter or a water vole.

Walking through the fens, especially on trails through reserves such as the RSPB Strumpshaw Fen Reserve, or the How Hill Nature Trail, you can encounter all of these animals and a lot more among the reeds and pools. In the spring and summer, wildflowers add swathes of colour to the scenery and muddy pools are graced with yellow irises and white water lilies.

Left:

a   A Norfolk Hawker dragonfly in flight

b   Meadow Brown and Gatekeeper butterflies throng on the wildflowers that line the Broads

c   A Swallowtail butterfly at Strumpshaw Fen (photo by Tim Melling)

d   A Yellow Flag Iris

e   An orchid, probably a hybrid of Common Spotted and Southern Marsh species

Right: A typical view in The Broads looking towards Brundall on the River Yare

Overleaf Left: Winter reed beds and swans at Hickling Broad

Overleaf Right: The view from How Hill over Reedham Marshes and the River Ant

The Northern Broads

North of the River Yare, the Broads, whose names are usually taken by the nearest village, are centred on the rivers Bure (Wroxham, Hoveton, Hickling and Ranworth Broads), Ant (Barton and Sutton Broads) and Thurne (Hickling and Martham Broads and Horsey Mere). The rivers wind through the countryside, sometimes opening into a lake, usually with reedy marshes on either bank. Lots of channels and creeks, some penetrating miles into the countryside, link stretches of water, providing a vast network of waterways for motor boats, yachts and canoes. They are so popular that most of the towns and villages have ships chandlers, extensive marinas and repair yards. Here you can buy or rent any type of boat that takes your fancy and head off on a real voyage of discovery through this unique landscape.

At boating centres like Wroxham, Horning and Brundall, boats of all sizes from canoes to large motor cruisers are lined up for hire when they are not gently exploring the waterways. In between voyages, you can moor the boat and relax on dry land, watching the endless comings and goings from the many pub verandas, cafes and parks

There are all sorts of treasures to be found on the way through the Broads, such as How Hill on the Ant (page 21) where the large thatched edifice of How Hill House perches on the top of the highest hill in the Broads at 40 feet (12 metres) above sea level. This is a field study centre with great views and an excellent nature trail that takes you through the marshes on good paths with great access to the wildlife. Alternatively you might explore the Fairhaven Woodland and Water Garden at South Walsham, or Hoveton Hall Gardens, or wander through tree canopies at BeWILDerwood near Ludham. Ludham is also hosts the Norfolk Wherry Trust so you quite likely to see one or two of these iconic boats around Womack Water which runs from the village to the River Yare.

Facing Page: Cottages at Hardley on the Yare

This Page: Some common Norfolk birds

a Chaffinches at a feeder
b Two Swallows
c A Robin
d A Pied Wagtail
e A Black-tailed Godwit among Black Headed Gulls
   at the WWT Welney Wetland Centre
f A Wren

Norwich and Central Norfolk

When the Normans were building the Cathedral and Castle a thousand years ago, Norwich was the second largest city in England, and it continued to thrive with weaving as its main industry for centuries. These days it is loved for being a compact city which is relatively easy to get around, with a good balance between heritage, culture and business. Although it was bombed in the war, a lot of beautiful historic buildings remain in very good condition, making it an interesting and attractive place to visit or live in.

The Castle, with its formidable square keep rising from its mound, dominates the city centre, offering great views across Norwich and serves as the city's museum.

Left: The Ethelbert Gate into the Cathedral Close. The Ethelbert Gate enters the Cathedral Close from Queen Street. It was built in 1316 after the original gateway and the nearby Anglo-Saxon church of St Ethelbert were destroyed during an uprising in 1272, when conflict arose between the local church and the citizenry. King Henry III punished the citizens, making them build the gate, including a chapel, in reparation for burning down the old church of St Ethelbert.

Right: Norwich Cathedral of the Holy and Undivided Trinity was founded in 1096 by Herbert de Losinga, who became the first Bishop. He acquired a lot of land at the centre of the ever growing town of Norwich that already contained two churches and many houses, but had them removed to make way for his cathedral, priory and other new buildings. His vision has left us this wonderful Cathedral Close, but at the cost of poor relations for many generations between the church and the town.

The precinct, or 'Close' as it is known, is the largest to survive in England. It contains many historic houses that make the Close attractive and interesting. There is also a large grassy sward where people can relax and enjoy the peace and calm in the midst of the busy city.

Overleaf Left: Norwich Market and the Guildhall. Right in the middle of Norwich by the County Hall, the covered market is one of the largest in Britain and has traded in this location since Norman times. The Guildhall at its eastern end is the largest medieval civic building in England outside London and served as the seat of city government from the early fifteenth century right up until 1938, when it was replaced by the City Hall.

Overleaf Right: Norwich Castle from Castle Mall

The River Wensum and Norwich

Norwich is situated at the confluence of the Rivers Wensum and Yare, but it is the former that flows through the City. It rises about 27 miles to the north-west and flows through Fakenham on its way to Norwich where it takes a loop around the Cathedral and City centre, passing under eighteen bridges on the way. It joins the River Yare quite close to the location of the image on the left, on the southwest edge of the city at Whitlingham Country Park. The Yare effectively defines the southern limits of Norwich before flowing eastwards towards The Broads, Great Yarmouth and the North Sea.

The River Wensum used to be the city's main transport link to the outside world, so until rail and road transport took over, its navigability was essential for moving people and goods efficiently. Nowadays it is mainly used for tourism, offering as it does a delightful scenic passage through Norfolk's heartland. This photograph was taken from the Carrow Bridge which is the lowest bridging point on the Wensum which will open to allow large ships to pass up river.

The ruins on either side of the river were 'boom towers' that there were once part of the medieval defences of Norwich; by night a chain was strung between them across the river to deter enemy ships (possibly Dutch at the time) from sailing in under cover of darkness.

Norfolk Mills

Approximately 150 mill houses remain in Norfolk, though only two (Letheringsett and Saxlingham Thorpe) still operate as water mills. Both have installed electrical milling equipment in order to continue the work they were designed for, whilst many other mills have become private houses. One such is Corpusty Mill, shown on the right, where milling finally ceased in 1965 but where the machinery including the heavy oil engine, seed crushers and milling machinery remain intact. The current owner is Roger Last who has not only developed a fabulous garden at the Mill, but is a co-author of a book called 'Norfolk Gardens and Designed Landscapes' which describes the great majority of the historic gardens and parks in the county (Windgather Press, 2013).

Corpusty Mill is situated on the River Bure which becomes one of the major Broads rivers below Wroxham.

Left: The River Wensum in the middle of Norwich
Right: Corpusty Mill

Overleaf Left: All Saints Church at Thwaite, on the Weaver's Way near Aldborough
Overleaf Right: View over the Wensum Valley from the churchyard of St Mary, Bylaugh

Most of the Norfolk countryside is agricultural with huge acreages of arable farming, interspersed with areas of forest and its famous Broads. As can be seen above on land just to the east of Downham Market and the Fens, the character of much of Norfolk is undulating rather than flat, an excellent topography for growing crops.

Underlying much of Norfolk is a bed of cretaceous chalk that starts at the Hunstanton cliffs and descends to the southeast. Through much of the county, this has been overlaid with more recent deposits including silt and peat in the western fens, soils that are sandy and acid in the southern Brecks or light and slightly calcareous in the northwest, clay through the middle and neutral loams or marshy broads in the east. The county would originally have been mostly covered in trees, but people started changing the landscape as long as 7,000 years ago, clearing the land and keeping livestock. Fields were mostly open, although much divided into strips, until the sixteenth century when enclosures commenced, partly driven by increased animal herding and more strongly by the Enclosure Acts of Parliament around 1800. During this period, large numbers of hedges were planted, dividing up the previously very open land and these remained in place, defining what we think of as 'typically English' countryside, until after the Second World War. In the quest for more efficient agriculture and increased food supply, up to 70,000 miles of hedges were destroyed in Norfolk alone between 1946 and 1980, completely altering the landscape and destroying a vast wildlife refuge which had, to an extent, replaced the forests.

The open rural landscape of Norfolk that we see today can be efficiently farmed using huge machines whose size is now limited only by the width of the roads, and even then all the traffic on the smaller lanes has to stop if it meets a combine harvester. One consequence is that the land has lost much of its character and natural history, contributing to the pressures on many bird, mammal and insect species.

That being said, the pace of life in rural communities can still be quite gentle and we see, on the left, that some Norfolk chaps have the time to spend a sunny Tuesday afternoon fishing in the village pond.

Left: A relaxed Tuesday afternoon at Wereham Pond
Above: Looking north towards Broughton over summer fields

Heydon

Heydon Hall is a lovely Elizabethan house, built in the 1580s, which has been owned by the Bulwer-Long family since 1762. It is situated in five hectares of park and gardens that comprise one of the finest examples of an unspoiled eighteenth century landscape in Norfolk. The park contains some huge and ancient oak and sweet chestnut trees along with a lake and a decorative folly tower.

Heydon village is all owned by the Bulwer family and has been conserved immaculately. It has no through road and no new building has been constructed there since a Jubilee well in 1887. This is situated on the huge village green, and is overlooked by the church of St Peter and St Paul which contains some very fine fifteenth-century wall paintings. It has a pretty teashop and an unspoilt pub, the Earle Arms which is named after the original inhabitants of the Hall.

Right: St Peter & St Paul's Church
Below: The tea shop and street of Heydon

The Common Poppy in the Norfolk Countryside

Common Poppy (*Papaver rhoeas*) was voted the County Flower of Norfolk when Plantlife organised a country-wide poll in 2002. These days it flourishes during summer months along roadsides and disturbed ground and occasionally you can find a field that has been taken over by them. Some countries use poppy seed in cakes and other recipes, but in England it is a weed that tends to be heavily controlled by farmers. Where it does thrive, however, it creates a vibrant spectacle that contrasts dramatically with white oxeye daisies and the familiar green of England.

The image on the left is a field verge looking towards the Church of St Margaret at Burnham Norton in the north of the county during a warm July. Clumps of poppies grow among the oxeye daisies in the verge surrounding a healthy, and poppy-free, wheat field. St Margaret's is a sizeable and well-built Norman church that belongs to the smallest of the Burnham group of villages, but in its quirky English way, it is much closer to Burnham Market than it is to the smaller village to which it belongs.

The image on the facing page is a field off the A148 near Fitcham in north Norfolk where poppies dominate the centre of the field, and the grassy strip on its edge seems to lead us to the settlement and the bottom of the valley. This field is adjacent to Abbey Farm which farms part of its land organically and every winter attracts many thousands of pink-footed geese for which the farm grows beets, whose green tops are a preferred food.

This landscape with its gentle hills and valleys and its modestly sized fields with rich hedgerows contrasts with the wide open countryside to the south and east.

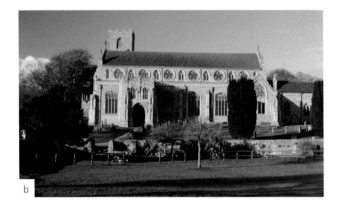

a

b

c

A Selection of Norfolk Churches

Norfolk has lots of churches of all sizes with quite a variety of designs. The most particular to Norfolk are probably those with round towers, but there are also many ancient buildings with square towers. The churches chosen for these pages are not necessarily the most interesting or beautiful, but have been selected from those that were photographed whilst researching this book to represent the main types. Those on this page include some smaller churches, round-, octagonal- and square-towers, and the three larger churches on the opposite page each has a particular point of interest or special feature.

a   St Mary, Bylaugh
b   St Margaret at Cley-next-the-Sea
c   St Mary, Beachamwell: thatched with a round tower
d   St Edmund, Downham Market, made of carrstone blocks
e   All Saints, Chedgrave
f   St Gregory, Heckingham: thatched with an octagonal tower
g   The 111-foot tall tower of St Peter and St Paul, Salle
h   St Mary Magdalene at Sandringham: The Queen's church is made of coursed carrstone
i   St Nicholas, Blakeney with its second, western, tower

d

e

f

South Norfolk: Breckland and the Waveney Valley

Breckland, or The Brecks, is a large area of very sandy soil stretching from Swaffham in the north, through Thetford and across the border into Suffolk towards Bury St Edmunds. The area has very light soil that is easily exhausted and as it is the driest part of England it was prone to sand storms in the past when high winds over the low terrain picked up the dry soil particles. These days, much of the land is forested, especially with Scots Pine, and farmers are taking much more care to nourish and keep the sandy soil.

Thetford, which is the Breckland's principal town has been a place of importance since the Iron Age because it is here that the ancient Icknield Way crosses the River Little Ouse. There are a number of these old 'ways' in England that were the main routes of travel from one end of the country to the other: the Icknield Way, possibly named from Boudica's Iceni tribe, once connected Norfolk (possibly from Great Yarmouth) with Salisbury in Wessex. King Cnut (Canute) was the last East Anglian king to sit at Thetford in the eleventh century, before the Norman conquest.

When the Normans came, they secured their conquered land with stone castles of which Thetford Castle, built in the twelfth century, was one. In the event, it didn't last long and was destroyed in 1173 by Henry II who was afraid that it would be taken over by restless locals. The huge man-made castle mound, or motte, is all that remains (seen on the right).

The town's most famous son was Thomas Paine, the political philosopher, activist and author of *The Rights of Man*, whose statue stands outside the Town Hall. Born in 1736 he started adult life as a corset maker, but left Thetford to pursue a mercurial life that took him into the company of George Washington, Ben Franklin and Napoleon, in between spells in prison, and rope making. His writings, putting persuasive arguments for all men to be treated equally, have influenced politicians throughout the centuries on both sides of the Atlantic. However his support for both the American and French revolutions whilst in those countries meant that he became viewed as a dangerous rabble-rouser at home, from which his reputation never recovered in some circles.

Other historic structures in Thetford include its ancient grammar school, which Paine attended, the Cluniac priory and a number of medieval and Georgian buildings, many with flint cladding.

Left: Thomas Paine's statue in Thetford
Right: Thetford Castle mound seen through the earth ramparts

The Other Statue: Captain Mainwaring

Much of the Dad's Army TV series was filmed in and around Thetford, so fans can find many of the well-known locations by following the Dad's Army Trail. The star attraction is probably the seated statue of Colonel Mainwaring on a bench by the river, where people can join him for a bit of contemplation, or even a quiet chat.

Thetford Forest

Thetford Forest starts at Thetford's western boundary and fans out to the north and west for some 10 miles across the gently rolling landscape. It is managed by the Forestry Commission and has extensive areas of broad-leaved forest, pine forest, heath, and a few arable farms. Although there are no ancient forests as these were chopped down a long time ago, the extensive plantations of trees are mostly mature offering many miles of delightful avenues to roam where a lot of wildlife is to be found. You can walk, ride or cycle along the many avenues and trails (see page 45), and during summer months these tend to be bordered by wildflowers among which bees and butterflies dance.

The heaths are the more traditional Breckland habitats, where views are open and, as well as plentiful rabbits, a number of uniquely Breckland species of wildlife can be found including stone curlews and woodlarks. One such area, just west of Weeting, is Cranwich Camp (page 44) which is now a nature reserve, but was built on in the 1930s as one of four labour-camps in Breckland. Inmates provided labour for forestry and other local projects until it was converted to military use during the war. Now, only a few Nissen huts and a type 22 hexagonal concrete pillbox remain from the Second World War. The heath itself is far, far older, the name 'Cranwich' being derived from an Old English word, 'cranes', meaning marshy meadow.

Weeting

On the western edge of Thetford Warren, just north of Brandon on the River Little Ouse is the village of Weeting, which boasts a round-towered church and a ruined 'castle' (actually a fortified manor). The main road through the village passes the longest terrace of thatch-roofed cottages in England, pictured on the left, fronted by the green and the village sign.

Left: The village sign and row of thatched cottages at Weeting
Right: Captain Manwaring's seated statue in Thetford attracts a companion

Overleaf Left: Cranwich Camp Heath on the edge of Thetford Forest
Overleaf Right: Cyclists on a ride through Thetford Warren

Twisted Pine Trees

The rows of twisted Scots pines along this road near the small village of Cockley Cley, pictured on the left, were managed as a hedge until well into the twentieth century. It is unusual to use pines for hedging as they naturally grow tall and straight with a single trunk, rather than bushy, so pine hedges were cut back hard each year to promote branching and keep them low. Pines were used for hedging in this area because they grow better on the poor sandy soils than more normal hedge species, such as hawthorn. Now that they have been left to grow, each has a unique and erratic shape, as the trunk divides very low down creating an interesting road verge. The Cockley Cley estate is one of the last land-owners to plant pine hedges in England.

Rows of closely spaced pines called 'deal rows' in local parlance, were also planted along field edges (see page 48), so rows of Scots Pine, twisted and straight, are quite a common sight in the Breckland region.

Lynford Arboretum

Very close to Weeting off the A1065 is Lynford Arboretum, which is connected with Lynford Hall. This is a Jacobean style mansion, built in the nineteenth century by a Mr Lynn Stephens and subsequently bought by the Forestry Commission in 1924 as a training establishment. The Commission planted trees throughout most of the estate, including the Arboretum, originally to provide trainees with a wide selection of different species as part of their education. Over two hundred tree species still grow in the Arboretum, which is open to the public and is a delightful location for a stroll and a picnic, whether or not one has an interest in arboreal botany. However, Lynford Hall is now a hotel that is independent of the Arboretum.

The County Border at Brandon

The county border with Suffolk lies along the middle of the River Little Ouse that rises south-west of Thetford and flows east to join the Great Ouse in the Fens. The town of Brandon lies in Suffolk, but there is a small extension north of the river that includes the railway station. The river is quiet nowadays, but a trade directory published in 1883 states: "A considerable trade is carried on in malt and timber and in fur and skin dressing. Barges ply to and from Lynn with corn and coal." The image on page 49 is taken from Brandon Bridge and shows how things have changed.

Left: A Breckland road near Cockley Cley, lined with twisted pines
Right: In Lynford Arboretum

Overleaf Left: A row of pines on an arable field boundary near Mundford
Overleaf Right: The River Little Ouse at Brandon, which forms the border with Suffolk

Above: The garden of the Twenty Churchwardens pub in Cockley Cley, with All Saints church in the background

Right: The River Wissey at Stoke Ferry

North Breckland Villages

Swaffham is a delightful market town that lies at the north end of Breckland. To its south, the light, free-draining soil in this relatively dry part of the country, combined with flints that endlessly rise from the underlying chalk makes farming difficult and yields poor. Trees don't mind these conditions, so large areas have been forested, mostly with pines, by the Forestry Commission in plantations such as Swaffham and Cockleycley Heaths.

One consequence of the low fertility of the land is that the human population is quite low and settlements are few and widely spread. South-east of Swaffham, between forests and heaths, lies Beechamwell, with its expansive cottage-lined village green and St Mary's Church. This is one of the prettiest churches in Norfolk with its round tower and thatched roof (see page 38).

A few miles further south-east, three other villages of North Breckland are located along the small River Gadder, which is the only waterway in the area. Sitting on its north bank, the first is Cockley Cley which was the location of an attempt to recreate an Iceni village as a living museum; the Iceni being the tribe that Boudica led in revolt against the Romans during the first century AD. The museum has gone, but the village has the Twenty Churchwardens Pub (named after a type of clay pipe) from whose garden the image on the left was taken. All Saints Church in the background unfortunately lost most of its round tower when it collapsed in 1991.

Following the river downstream to the south-west, is Gooderstone with its sturdy square-towered church of St George and the picturesque Gooderstone Water Gardens, which are open to the public. Then a mile further down the same brook lies Oxborough, which has a magnificent fifteenth-century moated hall. This was built by the Bedingfield family who still live there, although the house and gardens are now managed by the National Trust and are open to the public.

The River Gadder then joins the River Wissey a mile and a half to the south.

The River Wissey

The Wissey flows west from its source near Bradenham, then loops southwards, gently weaving through the Brecks. It skirts the north end of Thetford Forest, passing Mundford whose church of St Leonard also lost its tower through a collapse in the early 1900s, but which was later replaced by the current spire.

The image on the right is taken at Stoke Ferry at the very edge of Breckland, so called because the river has also been called the 'River Stoke' in the past. Although the scene looks familiar, the Wissey is not connected to the Norfolk Broads, but it does offer extensive waterways to explore as it flows east to join the River Great Ouse deep in the fens.

The Waveney Valley

The River Waveney rises a few miles west of Diss in Redgrave Fenn, which is also the location of the source of the Little Ouse which flows in the opposite direction. Both rivers form the boundary between Norfolk and Suffolk, which means that Norfolk is almost an island, joined only at this little fen. The Waveney passes through a gentle, pastoral landscape punctuated by a string of delightful little towns and villages that lend the area an individual character that is neither particularly Norfolk nor Suffolk. It is a slow-changing landscape, rooted in a long history that is revealed in its pre-Roman pastures, moated farms, ancient byways and hedgerows.

Unlike the Yare, which divides the country to its north and south, the Waveney is crossed by a number of bridges, so is not a major obstacle as a boundary. There are a few small but steep hills that provide excellent views across the countryside, particularly from the Suffolk towns of Beccles and Bungay. Another feature of the Waveney valley is the several lakes along its valley, but these are old gravel pits rather than peaty broads.

Historically the river became navigable at Bungay, where it takes a big loop around the rocky promontory on which the town sits, its little castle guarding the valley. These days boating starts a little further downstream, from which point the opportunities for navigation are many as there are now man-made channels that connect the Waveney to the Norfolk Broads and also to Lowestoft and the North Sea. Towards Beccles, the Waveney Valley broadens, becoming more marshy and broad-like before the river flows into Breydon Water at Burgh Castle.

There is a strong artistic tradition along the Waveney, with theatres and art galleries in the towns and artists' studios scattered along its valley. In July each year, during the Harleston and Waveney Arts Trail, the studios open their doors for a public celebration of art.

Below: The upper Waveney Valley near Brockdish
Right: A summer's evening below Scole

Overleaf Left: View across the Waveney near Harleston
Overleaf Right: Morning sunlight on the River at Ellingham Mill

Diss

Diss lies on the Norfolk bank of the River Waveney, a few miles from its source at Redgrave Fen. It is a thriving market town that also lies on the main railway line from Norwich to London. At its centre is the 14th century parish church of St Mary The Virgin and the market square (seen opposite) where a market is still held every Friday. The Mere (above) is a small lake, about 60 feet deep, not connected to the River Waveney. It lies in a natural depression, much of it taken up by silt now, but how that formed is a mystery that remains unresolved.

Above: The Mere with the parish church and central Diss beyond
Right: Diss Market Square with its 14th century parish church of St Mary The Virgin

West Norfolk and The Fens

The landscape in the western part of Norfolk is low-lying fenland that continues across much of Cambridgeshire and Huntingdonshire. The landscape really is totally flat and was once a vast marsh which was impossible to farm. In the seventeenth century, Francis Russell, the Earl of Bedford, decided to start draining the land using dykes and windmills, enlisting the help of Dutch engineers. Ever since then, agriculture has depended upon the huge channels, called drains, that take the water away from the land and out to The Wash. The fields are vast, the horizons distant and the skies enormous, and there are few hedgerows or woods to break up the monotony. There aren't many roads, and those that exist are rather odd, as they travel dead straight for a few miles, then suddenly take a sharp turn to run in a completely different direction. They are also bumpy because the underlying peat is an unreliable base that tends to subside.

The land is sparsely populated, with small isolated settlements separated by long acreages of low-lying arable and the occasional farm. Downham Market, situated on rising land above the River Great Ouse, is the only sizeable town associated with the fens apart from Kings Lynn, which lies at the fens' north-east limit. The Great Ouse empties into The Wash to the north from where the landscape becomes wooded and changes to the pretty and rather hilly landscape of North Norfolk.

At the other end of the fens, in the extreme south-east corner of Norfolk, lies the village of Welney, which is close to where the images on this page spread were taken. The Bedford River (opposite) runs dead straight in its two channels (Old and New) from Earith in Cambridgeshire to Denver Sluice (page 63) where it re-joins the River Great Ouse, which has taken a huge loop to the east from the same starting point.

Water management throughout the fens is done at an enormous scale, but without it this land would return to unproductive marshland, and many of its dwellings would be partially submerged. Some effects of not draining the land can be seen at Welney Wetland Centre, run by the Wildlife and Wetlands Trust, where the Lady Fen and some land on the other side of the Bedford have been allowed to return to their natural state. This has been done in order to encourage wetland birds, which can now be seen in considerable numbers on the open water and marsh. The Centre provides access by path to the lakes and bird hides and includes a permanent exhibition and a cafe.

Left: Lady Fen from the Welney Wildfowl & Wetlands Trust site
Right: The New Bedford River, or Hundred Foot Drain at Welney Wetlands Visitor Centre

Overleaf Left: Agricultural fenland at Methwold Common
Overleaf Right: View from Welney Bridge down the New Bedford River

Downham Market

To the east of the River Great Ouse, the ground begins to rise and the underlying material is rock rather than peat and other soggy sediments. Solid ground, combined with access to the Great Ouse as a waterway, made Downham Market a good location for a commercial centre servicing the Fens farms and villages. The local stone is a brown sandstone, called 'carr stone', which has been used to construct many of the buildings here and throughout West Norfolk. It is very characteristic of the area and its widespread use has resulted in Downham Market being named the 'Gingerbread Town'. The image of coursed carr stone below is part of the town hall.

The Denver Sluice

The Bedford River and several large drainage channels join the Great Ouse at this important water control system, comprised of a series of huge barriers and weirs. The system was originally conceived and built by a Dutch engineer called Cornelius Vermuyden in 1651 and improvements have continued ever since as technology has advanced. The Great Denver Sluice (shown on the right), built in 1964, is part of a system of several barriers across the various drains and rivers. These structures protect the Great Ouse from tidal water which, if allowed to pass, could introduce salinity and cause the water upstream to back up, flooding the fenland. Managing water on this scale is a prodigious undertaking, and over the years, many problems have been overcome in order to protect the land. Even today, the system requires constant maintenance and periodical upgrading of equipment.

Left: The clock tower in Downham Market's town centre
Below: Close-up of coursed carr stone in the Downham Market town hall wall
Right: One of the big dams at Denver Sluice

Overleaf Left: King's Lynn dockside
Overleaf Right: The statue of George Vancouver in front of the Custom's House at King's Lynn

King's Lynn

The image above is the view of King's Lynn from the A17 road bridge across the Great Ouse; the river that brought the trade that built the town. In the Middle Ages, 'Lynn' was England's third biggest port with ships docking from all over the North Sea and Baltic, helping make Norfolk one of the wealthiest counties. The 'King's' prefix dates from the Dissolution, when the entire town became the property of Henry VIII, and the connection was reinforced when it remained a Royalist stronghold during the Civil Wars.

The Lynn is packed with points of historic interest and beautiful buildings, and signs of its trading past can be seen along the riverside and in the warehouses lining the narrow streets of the old town. There are numerous churches and museums, stately terraces, pretty cottages dating from all historic periods and two large and ancient market squares; one active on Tuesdays and the other on Saturdays. It is a thriving commercial centre that is full of scenic and historic interest and well worth a visit.

The images on the previous pages show the South Quay and the seventeenth-century customs house, with George Vancouver's statue to the front. He was born in Lynn, the son of a customs officer who probably worked at this building. He was one of Britain's greatest explorers and navigators, charting new areas in the Pacific and also the Northwest Passage in the Canadian Arctic. He died in obscurity at the age of 40, but his achievements were later recognised when the city of Vancouver in Canada was named after him.

The Dragonflies of Norfolk

Through its many rivers, broads and fens, Norfolk possesses a lot of surface water with the unpolluted, muddy conditions that suit aquatic life. Combined with the relatively warm sunny weather, dragonflies abound in Norfolk and the County even has a few of its own. The Norfolk & Norwich Naturalists' Society lists 32 species that can be found, particularly in places like Welney WWT Centre in the western fens and, in the east, along the rivers and lakes of the Norfolk Broads. They thrive in the slow running water and can be seen dashing about in their erratic way during all the summer months. The names given to taxonomic groups of dragonflies, like 'darter', 'skimmer' and 'hawker' point to their behaviour in the air, but it is worth waiting quietly until they land when, if you are a bit lucky, you will be able to see their beautiful colouring, huge faceted eyes and four lacy wings.

Above: The River Great Ouse approaching King's Lynn with the towers of St Margaret's Church on the left

Right: Some Norfolk dragonflies:
a   Migrant Hawker
b   Common Darter
c   Southern Hawker
d   Black-tailed Skimmer
e   Emperor female laying eggs

a

b

c

d

e

Norfolk's West Coast and The Wash

At King's Lynn, the River Great Ouse empties into the shallow waters of The Wash, which is a square-shaped bay lying between Norfolk and Lincolnshire. Three other rivers also empty into The Wash, each depositing its silt, so the bay is becoming shallower and smaller as these sediments build up. This means that the land is growing, and King's Lynn that was once a sea port is now three miles inland along with the villages of Dersingham, Snettisham and Heacham to the north.

On the coast west of Snettisham, a new settlement, called Shepherd's Port has developed with a large holiday park and the enormous shingle beach pictured opposite. This is a coast of wide skies, a gentle sea and a sunny climate.

Heacham remains much closer to the sea and owing to its warm climate, is notable for Norfolk Lavender, pictured on the right. This image looks west over the main lavender field towards the village and the sea about a mile away. Nearby is the Norfolk Lavender Centre which has a lavender garden, tea shop, herb oil distillery and other activities.

A little south of Dersingham lies the royal estate of Sandringham which is one of the most popular visitor attractions in the country. The entire Estate spreads over 20,000 acres with a mixture of farms and the lovely park and gardens surrounding Sandringham House. It is a favourite residence of the Royal Family who visit frequently and attend the Church of St Mary Magdalene which is also within the Estate (see page 38). The house and gardens are open to the public from April to October whilst the park and visitor centre are open all year.

Although the coastal landscape is quite flat, the land rises to the east of the main road onto the rather hilly terrain of the chalk downs.

Left: The beach near Snettisham
Right: Norfolk Lavender in bloom at Heacham

North Norfolk

The final section of this book traverses the spectacular North Norfolk coast from Hunstanton on The Wash in the west to Cromer in the east where the North Sea batters the cliffs. This is one of the driest and sunniest parts of Britain, causing lovers of Hunstanton to call it 'Sunny Hunny'. Along the entire coast the light has a special quality which seems to bring alive the colours of the awe-inspiring open vistas across marsh, dune and sea. Along the main A149 road which follows the coast lies a string of pretty villages, several of which have the words 'next-the-sea' in their names, and all have a staithe, or quay. However, they are actually a little inland these days as the North Sea has been steadily removing sand, pebbles and silt from cliffs along the East Coast of England, depositing them here, on the southern side of The Wash. The result is that the beaches have gradually migrated northwards leaving the settlements stranded up to two miles inland behind acres of dunes and salt marshes that are crossed only by shallow channels linking the staithes to the open sea.

This is a landscape where geese, ducks and wading birds flock in their thousands and the light shimmers off water and mud. It is a unique place that people adore for sailing, walking, bird watching, crabbing, or just relaxing. In contrast, there are the seaside towns at either extremity of Hunstanton in the west and Cromer in the east, each with its beach, beach huts, hotels and shops, not forgetting Cromer's majestic pier. The pretty flint-clad villages in-between, each with its own character, separate the hilly hinterland from the vast level marshes.

The north is the hilliest part of Norfolk, rising to the County's highest point of 103 metres (338 ft) at Beacon Hill, a few miles south of Sheringham. This is a varied and pretty landscape where sizeable forests and heath land are interspersed with farms and a number of large estates and country houses.

Below: Looking east along the north coast on a windy day. The image is taken from Cley Eye, at the east end of Blakeney Point. Sheringham is on the headland in the distance, from where the coast starts to turn southwards

Right: A channel at Burnham Overy Staithe

Hunstanton Cliffs

Hunstanton is a pleasant seaside town that came to prominence in Victorian times and remains popular today. It is much more sheltered than Cromer or Sheringham at the other end of this coast and has a quite different appearance because its most typical buildings are constructed of red carrstone, rather than being flint-clad. At low tide, the beach is a vast stretch of fine sand which seems to go on forever out to the shallow sea.

Just north of the town, at Old Hunstanton, the beach is backed by the unique and colourful banded cliffs. On the top is a deep layer of white chalk, which is the bedrock of this area, and then there is an abrupt transition to chalk that is stained a bright brick red by minerals. At the base of the cliff the rock is the hard brown carrstone traditionally used for building houses. Chalk is a sedimentary rock resulting from countless microscopic marine organisms (diatoms) with hard shells falling to a shallow sea floor over millions of years, then getting compacted into rock that is almost pure calcium carbonate. This is normally white and how the sudden colour transition from white to red came about is unexplained.

Great lumps of cliff are constantly falling off as the sea pounds the soft rock, leaving ledges where fulmars nest.

Above: A pair of Fulmars nesting on the cliff face

Right: A close-up of the two types of chalk showing the sudden transition from white to red

Facing Page: A view of the banded cliffs

The Western Part of the North Coast

From St Edmund's Point, north-east of Hunstanton, the banded cliffs end, to be replaced by sand dunes, which these days are speckled with colourful beach huts. The dunes continue for many miles, protecting the low-lying marsh and farmland behind them from the pounding North Sea waves and tides. Where dunes have not formed, such as along encroaching channels, salt marshes have been created where reeds, samphire and curlews thrive.

The first village after Hunstanton is Holme-next-the-Sea, which, along with neighbouring Thornham and Tichwell, is a good mile inland nowadays. Most houses are constructed of 'clunch', which is a hard chalky rock that gives the houses a quite different appearance from those further to the east. (see page 97).

At Holme and at Titchwell there are nature reserves reached by tracks from the villages, where the salt marshes, the freshwater lakes and the beach beyond are all wonderful locations from which to watch birds. Gulls, terns and sanderlings comb the beach for food among the breaking waves, whilst a few yards away, all manner of ducks and waders, including avocets, stalk across the shining mud on spindly legs, stabbing it with their long beaks in the search for hidden delicacies. Great stretches of the marshes are covered in samphire, a succulent plant that copes with the harsh, salty conditions and which has become quite popular in restaurants as a salad vegetable. The less marginal areas are covered in reeds where bitterns, buntings and warblers hide and call.

From Titchwell, the A149 coast road continues in an easterly direction towards Sheringham through a series of picturesque villages that have become very popular as holiday destinations for yacht enthusiasts and those who love the open salt marsh scenery and its wildlife. Apart from Wells-next-the-Sea, the staithes are separate from the main settlement because of the marshes and these days are used for leisure rather than commercial fishing. The exception is Brancaster Staithe where mussels and whelks are still harvested and landed. The views over the salt marshes out towards the distant sea are unparalleled in a light that seems to sharpen the colour of small boats strewn across the mud and the channels and in the summer there is often a purple glow from stretches of sea lavender in flower. Throughout the winter, huge flocks of geese and other wading birds sail across the sky and gather in spectacular flocks in the marshes.

Open spaces and mud are not for everybody, so Wells and Burnham Market are very popular, offering plenty of attractive shops and eating places (see pages 86 and 99). South of the main road, the 'Downs' rise gently through farmland to about 180 feet and from the top, at places like Barrow Common, you are treated to some excellent panoramic views along the coast.

Left: A channel in the Titchwell Marsh RSPB reserve with Shelducks feeding in the mud
Right: The National Trust Tower Windmill at Burnham

Overleaf Left: Beach huts among the sand dunes at Old Hunstanton
Overleaf Right: The view over Brancaster from Barrow Common

Brancaster and Burnham Overy Staithe

At Brancaster and Brancaster Staithe, buildings start to become flint-clad, and this remains the style as you head east along the north coast. The two hotels and many holiday homes for rent cater for visitors but there is still a fishery, and Brancaster Staithe is used by commercial boats. These have to weave through miles of channels to reach their shellfish-beds in the expanse of Brancaster Harbour, and the open sea at Brancaster Bay beyond. For visitors, however, there is a much easier route, which is to drive or walk along a lane to the sandy beach less than a mile north of the village.

Scolt Head Island lies between Brancaster and the sea and has another bird reserve and a large beach which can be reached by a ferry from the staithe. On the mainland, just to the east of the main village are the remains of Branodunum, a Roman fort and settlement that was also a Saxon stronghold against invaders from the sea.

The next village is Burnham Deepdale with its pretty round-towered church that contains an ancient stone font. A bit further east lie the other Burnhams: Burnham Overy Staithe, Burnham Town, Burnham Ulf, Burnham Norton, Burnham Market, and Nelson's birth place at Burnham Thorpe. Burnham Overy Staithe looks out onto boat-strewn channels and is a favourite with the yachting fraternity; in fact sailing is such a focus here that there is a chandlery but no cafe or pub, although both can be found close by on the main road. For walkers, the Norfolk Coastal Path follows the edge of the marshes to Brancaster in one direction, and to Wells in the other across the sandy expanse of Holkham Bay.

Burnham Market, which is the largest of the group of villages and has become very smart with its restaurants, galleries and boutique shops, feels a little like Chelsea-near-the-Sea. However neighbouring Burnham Overy Town and the other Burnhams are tiny and consist only of a few buildings and some picturesque churches.

Below: Samphire growing in the mud of Brancaster marshes on a dull, damp day
Right: Burnham Overy Staithe at low tide

The huge expanse of sands at
Holkham Bay

Holkham

Holkham village is situated on the A148 and comprises of the Victoria Hotel and a few houses that lead to the gates to Holkham Park. At one time there was a landing with access to the sea, but a lot of the marshland was reclaimed by Holkam Estate so nothing remains these days of the staithe. From the car park at Holkham, it is a short walk through pine-clad dunes to the beach where sand stretches as far as the eye can see under the enormous sky, out to the breaking waves. Between the beach and the pines are marshy stretches where samphire, sea lavender and other saltmarsh plants colour the mud below. It is often a windy place and the gulls wheel and soar in the air, whilst the sand is sculpted into odd shapes around the scattered pebbles and shells. It is possible to walk for miles along the coastal path under the ever-changing sky, towards Wells to the east or to Burnham Overy Staithe to the west.

Holkham Hall is one of the principal Palladian houses of England. It was built by the 1st Earl of Leicester in the eighteenth century and remains today the home of the Coke family. The Earl took great pride in his creation, installing a seat at a prime viewing point, in order to keep an eye on the progress of building works. The photograph below was taken at this point, showing how the park and lake were landscaped to show off the Hall to its best advantage. The column rising from the centre of the building is actually about a mile behind it, but seems to have been placed with great care so that it appeared at the apex of the hall entrance when viewed from the south. The Hall and grounds are open to the public who can enjoy the herds of deer roaming through the park-land scenery, perhaps visiting the temple, the great barn and the thatched ice-house that lie within the park.

Left: Heading east along Holkham Beach
Below: Holkham Hall and Lake

Wells-next-the-Sea

In reality, Wells is near, rather than 'next' the sea and is a very charming little town with flint-clad buildings that line narrow, picturesque streets leading to the lively staithe. The name 'Wells' is derived from fresh springs that once percolated up through the glacial chalk of this stretch of coast, the rest of the name being added much later.

It has been a port and shipyard for at least 700 years, peaking in the nineteenth century when coal, timber and salt were the chief imports and grains were exported on the ships docking here. The other main industry was making malt for beer and some of the many granaries and maltings still exist, though most have been converted to other uses. The most prominent building on the quay is the large granary building with its distinctive overhanging gantry, which can be seen on the right had side of the image on this page.

Since then, storms and the expansion of the marshes due to silt deposits have resulted in the quay becoming only usable only by small vessels. There is still a small crab fishery and a lively trade in crab lines and buckets that can be hired by holiday-makers to fish from the quay. The image opposite shows a pile of crab creels alongside some intent amateurs trying their luck, and the main channel heading out towards the sea, over a mile away. For those without a boat, a miniature railway plies to and fro along the dyke between the town and the beach where there is a lifeboat station and lively array of stilted beach huts.

Moored against the quay at Wells is the 'Albatros' (left), which is an oddly named 100-year-old Dutch clipper that is now used as a sort of pub, where the visitor can drink, eat and even stay overnight.

The town, which extends about a mile inland, once had a great many pubs catering for the many sailors, fishermen and other sea-faring visitors arriving and leaving from the busy port. There are fewer pubs now, but Wells remains well supplied with hotels, shops and restaurants. Staithe Street, pictured overleaf, is great fun to stroll along, although it can get very busy in the holiday season.

Left: The Albatros: a 100-year old Dutch clipper that now serves as a pub moored at Wells

Right: The staithe at Wells-next-the-Sea with crab pots and a family fishing for crabs with lines

Overleaf Left: Staithe Street in Wells-next-the-Sea
Overleaf Right: The back of a pub at the end of Staithe Street

Birds of the North Norfolk Salt Marshes

The marshes of the North Norfolk coast have grown and spread over the years and caused the demise of the fishing and shipping that used to sustain the communities ranged along it. However, the area has become an astonishingly rich haven for native and migrating birds who thrive in the nutrient rich marshy landscape. Over 420 species have been recorded in Norfolk, including resident species, breeding and winter visitors, passage migrants and many vagrants, some of which have become very rare.

There are many opportunities for people to enjoy the spectacle of huge flocks of geese and other birds, winging across the sky, or landing to roost and feed. This is best done from bird hides strategically placed in the Cley and Titchwell reserves, but a lot can often be seen during a stroll along the Coast Path or while sitting quietly and watching. One bird can look much like another from a distance, so it is a good idea to take a pair of binoculars with you.

A few of the marsh specialists are shown here.

a   An Avocet
b   A Sandpiper
c   A Lapwing
d   A Redshank
e   A Curlew
f   Three Brent Geese

a

b

c

d

e

f

Left: A flock of Sanderlings take off into the wind on Cley Marshes RSPB Reserve, whilst Oyster Catchers wait in the foreground

Blakeney and Cley-next-the-Sea

Blakeney has the best of all the ingredients of a coastal Norfolk village: it is picturesque with its flint-pebble houses on quaint streets; there is the magnificent church of St Nicholas at the top of the village; it has a proper quay with a good-size channel for boats and a view over marshes thronging with birds. It also has the Blakeney Hotel which is a luxurious place to stay, right on the front from whose wide windows one can watch the weather and the birds in supreme comfort. There is a good footpath to Cley that keeps mostly to dry ground as it crosses the marshes towards the sea and then curls back towards its destination. This walk following one of the winding channels with views out towards Blakeney Point gives you a real feel for the marshes. The footpath doesn't quite reach the sea, but turns back inland where the River Glaven flows into the bay, with the shingle of the Point rising on the other side. The landward views approaching Cley are gorgeous with the sails of the windmill in the foreground and wooded hills rising behind.

Cley-next-the-Sea, with its landmark windmill (where you can also stay in great comfort), is similar to Blakeney but smaller, and the staithe is more diminished so the focus tends to be on wildlife and walking. There is another lovely church that was admired by John Betjeman, a good pub, some shops and lots of nooks and crannies to explore. Just to the east of the village is the Norfolk Wildlife Trust centre with information about the wildlife and a cafe looking out across the marshes. Here tickets can be bought to visit the hides on its marsh reserve and get close to the flocks of birds inhabiting the pools and reed beds.

Above: Blakeney Staithe
Right: Looking out along one of the marsh channels towards Blakeney Point and the sea: the building is known as 'Halfway House' as it is half way along the Point

Overleaf Left: Cley-next-the-Sea from the marsh footpath to Blakeney
Overleaf Right: Looking west across Morston Salt Marshes

Blakeney Point

Blakeney Point, like Scolt Island to the west, is a place where new land is being built from the silt and pebbles torn from the rapidly-eroding soft alluvial cliffs further up the English east coast. It starts at the car park at Cley Eye and runs roughly northwest in a straight line for about 4 miles (6 kilometres). It is composed of piles of sand and shingle, but the sand tends to sink down whilst the pebbles remain on the surface forming a shingle bank up to 10 metres in height. The majority of pebbles are flint, which goes some way to explaining why so many buildings in this region are flint-clad.

The end of the Point can be reached either by boat from Morston Quay or by walking its length from Cley Eye, in which case you need to be quite fit as shingle saps the energy, but is the only surface for much of its length. However the views can make it well worth the effort, with the bonus of colonies of grey seals and lots of sea birds amongst the pounding waves. For the first 3 miles, Blakeney Point is narrow with the wide expanse of Blakeney Channel separating it from the marshy land to the south, but towards the western end it broadens out forming a sort of claw of sand dunes. This wild landscape, where you can feel very close to nature and the elements, is protected by the National Trust.

Facing Page: Looking west along Blakeney Point from close to the car park at Cley Eye

Below: Geese in an arable field near Morston

Village Character in North Norfolk

Traditional building materials

As has already been described, older Norfolk towns and villages often derive their strong character from the very bedrock of their location in the County. Until recent times, people used local materials which differ greatly in their appearance and properties to build their homes, creating a characteristic regional look. In the west of Norfolk it is hard, brown carrstone which is a cretacious sandstone rock stained with varying amounts of iron oxide, and because of its appearance it is often called 'gingerbread stone'.

Flint cladding is common through much of north Norfolk and particularly along the North Coast from the Burnhams eastward. Flint is a very hard and durable rock which, once embedded in mortar, makes an erosion-resistant surface. The abundance of flints has a downside in that they are a severe nuisance for farmers as they constantly rise to the soil surface from the chalk below and damage farm machinery.

Chalk is not often used for buildings as it is too soft and dissolves in rainwater. There is, however, a more durable form called 'clunch' that is an attractive stone that has been used in many of the older buildings beteen Thornham and Kings Lynn.

Village Signs

Norfolk villages take great pride in their pictorial village signs, attempting to encapsulate what is special about the place. This tradition probably started in Norfolk early in the twentieth century when Edward VII wanted to make Sandringham more distinctive for visitors and create a new point of interest.

Left: Village signs:
Blakeney has an old fashioned sailing ship, a fiddler and a dog
Stiffkey shows people harvesting grain within a conch shell, a pig and a cup
Thornham has the staithe, a windmill and is surmounted by a model of the church
Wells-next-the-Sea shows an anchor, a fishing boat, pine trees and a sandy beach with bucket and spade

Facing Page:
Top Left: A house made of chalky clunch in Thornham
Top Right: A row of carrstone houses in Downham Market with a small brick property sandwiched in the middle
Lower Right: The flint-clad Three Horseshoes pub in Warham, along with the village sign

Village Character in Norfolk – The Businesses

One of the nice things about Norfolk villages and smaller towns is the range of locally owned businesses along the high streets whose appearance and stock reflects the owner's character rather than a multi-national brand. These butchers, bakers, tailors, teashops, hardware stores, galleries and so on not only reflect the nation's love of small enterprise, but are full of local colour and great fun to browse in. The few shown here are a sample of these little businesses that may catch the visitor's eye whilst travelling through the county. Burnham Market, below, is very attractive with interesting shops and eateries, many of which wouldn't be out of place in Chelsea. Perhaps more down-to-earth is the nearby town of Holt, which has a more local feel and is the commercial centre for the area's businesses and farms. It is an ancient town that already had a market at the time of the Domesday Book, but had to be rebuilt following a devastating fire in 1708. Most of the buildings towards its centre date from this time, contributing to Holt's individual character.

Left: Shop fronts in Holt, Wells and Bungay
Below: On Burnham Market Place

Behind the North Coast: Parks, Woods, Hills and a Railway

A holiday in North Norfolk has more to offer than beaches and salt marshes as the area just to the south is the hilliest in the whole of East Anglia and full of interest. The hills between Cromer and Holt are well forested in contrast to the flat coastal expanses elsewhere. Walking the paths over Beacon Hill (103 metres above sea level) and Stone Hill, the woods are mature and peaceful. They occasionally give way to areas of sandy heath, where heather and gorse thrive instead of trees, offering views northwards to the coast and the sea.

There are several large estates that are open to the public, such as Sheringham Park, Felbrigg Hall (both National Trust), Bayfield Hall, Holkham Hall and Sandringham offering gardens, wildlife and heritage. Sheringham Park is an undulating expanse of oak forest and meadow, and if you have the strength to climb through the dense oak wood to the top of the 'Gazebo', you look out over the tree canopy to the North Norfolk Railway line to Weybourne windmill, Cley Marshes and the sea.

Felbrigg Hall is a seventeenth-century house with extensive gardens that are beautifully maintained by the National Trust. It also has a park that continues into the Great Wood with tracks penetrating deep into the attractive mixed woodland. Here, goldcrests and woodpeckers are busy in the trees and colourful fungi swell in the damp leaf litter.

Further south, near Aylsford, Blickling Hall is another magnificent house with a lake and formal gardens that has been owned by the National Trust since 1940. It was built in the early 17th century, replacing the previous medieval building where Ann Boleyn was born.

A five-mile long railway known as 'the Poppy Line' was restored by volunteers in the 1960s and now runs a regular train service, often using heritage trains, from Sheringham to Holt. The line also offers special excursions powered by rare steam engines.

A few miles to the west, the Wells and Walsingham Light Railway runs between the two towns that give it its name. Unlike the Poppy Line, this is a small narrow-gauge railway, but it still manages to provide a regular service.

Left: The entrance to Blickling Hall
Right: A ride in Felbrigg Great Wood, near Sheringham

Overleaf Left: A steam train on the North Norfolk Railway (or the Poppy Line), from Sheringham Park

Overleaf Right: On Beacon Hill, the highest point in Norfolk

The Sheringham Coast

A big problem for much of the east coast of England is that the land is mostly soft sedimentary rock that is easily eroded and the North Sea is often very stormy and rough. Huge waves frequently undermine the cliffs causing landslides, the rubble from which is quickly turned to sand and mud by the sea and, in this case, redistributed to the salt marshes to the west. Sheringham perches on such a cliff and therefore has been protected by strong groins on the beach and a solid sea wall that is capped by a promenade wide enough to accommodate beach huts. People take great pride in these sometimes turning the interiors into a little exhibit for the many passers-by.

West Runton does not have such defences and the rate of cliff erosion here and all along the coast has necessitated the dumping of huge granite boulders to disrupt the sea's erosive power.

Left: The Promenade at Sheringham, heading east towards West Runton
Right: Some of these beach huts are displayed with pride
Below: Huge granite boulders on the beach at West Runton to protect the soft cliffs

Cromer

Cromer is principally a holiday town that developed from a fishing port in the nineteenth century, when it was very fashionable. It is still popular with visitors for its long sandy beaches, pier and seaside fun. From Sheringham eastwards, the salt marshes and mud are replaced by sandy beaches and clean sea close to the towns for those preferring a beach holiday to yachting or birding.

Cromer has had a pier or landing stage since the Middle Ages, but the current 140 metre (450 feet) pier was built in 1902. It was refurbished by North Norfolk Council in 2013, and now has the Pavillion Theatre which puts on shows and concerts throughout the year. The public can stroll along the walkways, enjoy a beer, or cast crabbing lines in the hope of a catching one of the famous Cromer crabs for dinner.

The off-shore lifeboat station is housed at the end of the pier with a steep ramp descending to the sea to launch the boat (see overleaf). There is also an inshore lifeboat, along with some traditional clinker-built fishing boats, housed next to the pier in the maritime heart of the town. The lifeboats are at the core of Cromer's character as they are essential for saving lives along this stormy coast and crewed by men who carry out heroic tasks, considering them as normal. The RNLI Museum is named after the greatest of these, Henry Blogg.

Crabs caught around Cromer have a reputation for excellence, and crab boats still go out fishing from Cromer, Sheringham and Runton, all of which are well furnished with good fish shops and restaurants. In May, there is also an annual crab festival held jointly with Sheringham.

The theme of locally owned businesses continues in Cromer, whose website, at the time of writing, claims: "In Cromer you will find a vibrant Norfolk town with a wide variety of cafes, restaurants, shops and accommodation, all independently owned and many passed down through the ages from parents to children."

Left: The beach looking west from Cromer cliff
Right: Looking across the sea front at Cromer

Overleaf: Views of Cromer Pier

Page 110: Sunset on Stiffkey Marshes

Index of Place Names

Acknowledgements

The Photographs

All images in this book are photographs that I took at the actual locations apart from the swallowtail butterfly on page 18. For this, I am very grateful to Tim Melling who works for the RSPB and also is a guide on amazing wildlife tours (look him up on Flickr.com).

The National Trust owns, manages and protects many heritage buildings and swathes of our best countryside including Blakeney Point and Nature Reserve, Brancaster Beach, Sheringham Park, Blickling, Felbrigg Hall and Oxburgh Hall which are included in this book. I am a registered National Trust Photographer and if you want to know more about the Trust, visit www.nationaltrust.org.uk.

A number of the images of waders and dragonflies were taken from within RSPB reserves at Strumpshaw Fen and Titchwell Marsh. They do wonderful work in enabling people to wander through the marshy landscapes and observe nature's many wonders: http://www.rspb.org.uk/discoverandenjoynature/seenature/reserves/.

Other images were taken in the World Wetlands Trust centre at Welney: http://www.wwt.org.uk/wetland-centres/welney/.

Also at How Hill, where the How Hill Trust provide environmental courses and a wonderful trail through the woods and marshes. It's worth a visit just to see the views and the extraordinary thatched How Hill House: http://howhilltrust.org.uk/.

The image on page 69 is by kind permission of Norfolk Lavender trading Ltd, Caley Mill, King's Lynn, Norfolk, PE31 7JE.

Research and References

During the early days of collecting material for this book, I read about the county of Norfolk in books and online, and also talked to friends who knew it well. I started designing my visits after reading Bradt's *Slow Travel in Norfolk* by Laurence Mitchell (Bradt Travel Guides Ltd, ISBN 978-1-84162-551-5), returning to it many times for guidance on places to visit and background information.

Hedgerow History by Gerry Barnes & Tom Williamson (Windgather Press, 2006, ISBN 978-1-905119-04-2) was helpful on understanding the geology of Norfolk and also the way in which the landscape developed.

Also helpful was *Norfolk Gardens and Designed Landscapes* by Dallas, Last and Williamson (Windgather Press, 2013, ISBN 978-1-905119-92-9).

I accessed a great many websites along the way, often starting with Google and Wikipedia. The Norfolk Churches Site (http://www.norfolkchurches.co.uk/) was particularly helpful in finding information about those I had photographed.

Proof reading is always a challenge and no matter how many times it is done, something always seems to slip through. I am particularly grateful to John Kedzierski, who brought his knowledge of linguistics and attention to detail to bear on the text, with the result that I was able to improve its elegance as well as correcting spelling and punctuation.

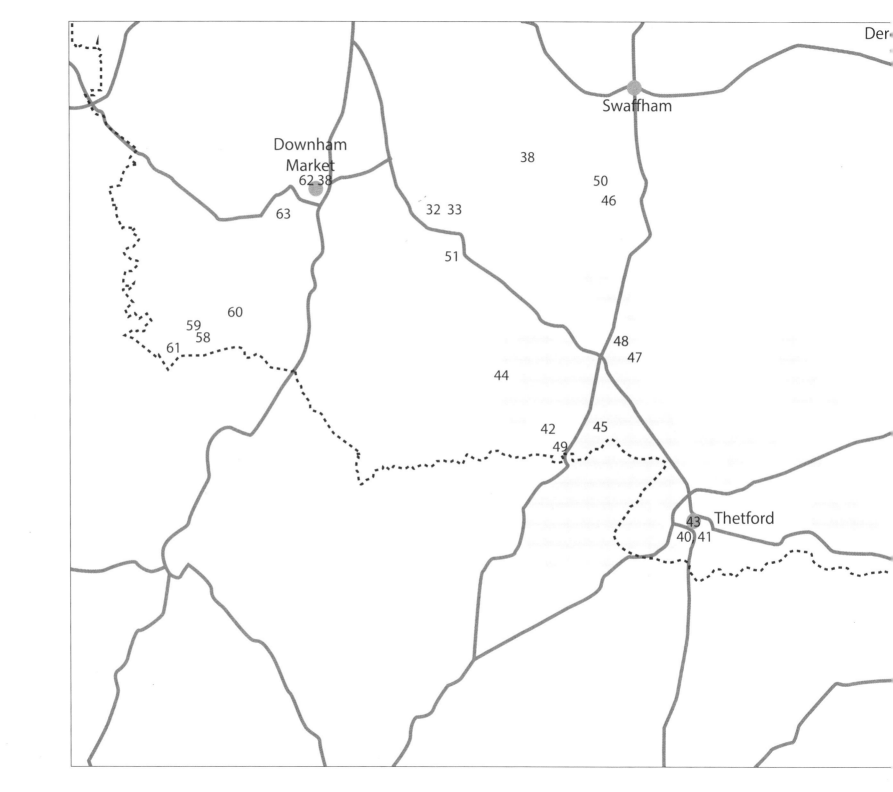